A Bible Study Guide on God's Statutes, Commandment and Judgments

Top 45 Bible Questions

N. Steele, R.N., M.P.H.

HEALMS Institute

Contents

OTHER BOOKS AVAILABLE

*How to Take Charge of Your
Colds, Flu & Lung Infection*

Sabbath Treasures

Ultimate Guide to Herbal Therapy fo Women

God's True Remedies

"Pure air, sunlight, abstemiousness, rest, exercise, proper diet, the use of water, trust in divine power—these are the true remedies. Every person should have a knowledge of nature's remedial agencies and how to apply them.""Counsels on Health" by Ellen G. White, Chapter 2,□

God has given us the true remedies by which we should live. When applied fully we not only follow his commands but through divine intervention attain healing both physically and spiritually. By following these remedies, fresh pure air, sunlight, being moderate in all things, adequate rest, physical activity, nutritious diet, water, and trust in God, we avail ourselves to his w ill.

Optimum Nutrition

The necessity of consuming a plant-based diet rich in fruits, vegetables, grains, and nuts is important for proper nutrition. This type of diet encourages both physical and mental well-being and should exclude meat and items that have undergone extensive processing. Overindulgence can be hurtful to the system therefore moderation in eating is encouraged.

A plant-based diet high in fruits, vegetables, whole grains, legumes, and nuts can have a number of positive effects on your health, according to multiple scientific research. A diet like this is linked to a lower risk of chronic illnesses, such as heart disease, stroke, type 2 diabetes, and several cancers. Additionally, it can aid in weight control and advance general well-being.[1]Limiting your intake of red and processed meats can reduce your risk of obesity, colon cancer, heart disease, and other illnesses. Dietary fiber is quite well-sourced in whole plant diets. Fibre is recognized to help with weight management because it supports digestive health, controls blood sugar levels, lowers cholesterol, and increases satiety. Scientific studies continuously emphasize the value of dietary fiber-rich foods.

Drinking pure, clean water is advised. Since water is involved in so many biological processes, such as digestion, circulation, and temperature regulation, being hydrated is crucial for general health. Highly processed foods are consistent with current health concerns over the dangers of consuming too much processed and ultra-processed meals, which frequently have extra sugars, bad fats, and preservatives.

"Grains, fruits, nuts, and vegetables constitute the diet chosen for us by our Creator. These foods, prepared in as simple and natural a manner as possible, are the most healthful and nourishing. They impart a strength, a power of endurance, and a vigor of intellect that are not afforded by a more complex and stimulating diet.""Counsels on Diet and Foods" by Ellen G. White, Chapter 1,□

<u>Optimum Nutrition List</u>
Whole Grain Foods:

1. Brown rice

2. Whole wheat bread

3. Whole wheat pasta

4. Quinoa

5. Oats (steel-cut oats, rolled oats)

6. Barley

7. Bulgur

8. Farro

9. Millet

10. Buckwheat

11. Teff

12. Amaranth

13. Spelt

14. Whole grain couscous

Legumes:

1. Lentils

2. Chickpeas (garbanzo beans)

3. Black beans

4. Kidney beans

5. Pinto beans

6. Navy beans

7. Split peas

8. Mung beans

9. Soybeans (edamame)

10. Fava beans

11. Black-eyed peas

12. Cannellini beans

13. Lima beans

14. Red beans

15. Adzuki beans

Nuts:

1. Almonds

2. Walnuts

3. Cashews

4. Pecans

5. Hazelnuts

6. Pistachios

7. Macadamia nuts

8. Brazil nuts

9. Pine nuts

10. Peanuts (technically legumes)

Seeds:

1. Chia seeds

2. Flaxseeds (ground or whole)

3. Sunflower seeds

4. Sesame seeds

5. Hemp seeds

6. Poppy seeds

7. Quinoa seeds

Physical Activity

The value of consistent exercise is important. Everyday activity, such as brisk walking outside, to keep one's health in check and ward off illness should be encouraged as this keeps the system working at its optimum level.

"Exercise aids the dyspeptic by giving the digestive organs a healthy tone. It assists the bowels in their work, and in this way the poor, overtaxed stomach has a chance to recover. The more we exercise, the better will be the circulation of the blood. More nerve force will be generated; all the organs will act more harmoniously, and the more easily will all physical difficulties be overcome." "Counsels on Diet and Foods" by Ellen G. White, Chapter 22,□

Research has shown that exercise is crucial in improving the cardiovascular system. It has been demonstrated that regular exercise, particularly physical activity, walking cycling, and swimming, improves cardiovascular health. It can lower blood pressure, enhance cholesterol profiles, and lessen the risk of heart disease. Strengthening the heart through exercise increases its ability to pump blood more effectively and improves circulation.

Exercise is essential for managing weight. It promotes lean muscle mass development and calorie burning. Regular physical activity can help with weight loss or weight maintenance when accompanied by a nutritious diet, lowering the risk of obesity-related illnesses including type 2 diabetes.

By strengthening the body's defense systems and promoting immune cell circulation, moderate, regular exercise helps strengthen the immune system. Moderation is crucial because prolonged, vigorous activity might temporarily weaken the immune system.

Numerous studies have demonstrated a significant correlation between consistent exercise and a longer life expectancy. A longer, better life is a result of exercise, lowered risk of chronic diseases, and improved general health.

Physical activity has been instrumental in powering the mind. As humans, we are faced with so many stressors on a daily basis. This constant bombardment of stressors can have a negative toll on mental health.

"Those who would have physical strength must use the physical powers. Those who would have mental strength must use the mental powers. Those who would have moral strength must use the moral powers." "The Ministry of Healing" by Ellen G. White, Chapter 20□

Increased mental health is demonstrated when exercise becomes a regular part of your life. The benefits of exercise for mental health are significant. Endorphins, which are naturally mood enhancers and can lessen the symptoms of anxiety and depression, are stimulated throughout this process. A lower risk of neurodegenerative disorders like Alzheimer's and higher cognitive function are both linked to regular physical activity.

Water Intake

For optimal health, pure, clean water must be used for drinking, bathing, and other activities. It is best to refrain from drinking alcoholic beverages. The effects on your organs, particularly your liver, may be negative. Adequate water consumption keeps the body well hydrated and cleanses it.

Life depends on water, and it has several advantages besides just keeping us hydrated. Some of the main advantages of water for general health and well-being are listed below:

Hydration is the most fundamental advantage of water. The body needs to be well hydrated in order to function normally. Our cells, tissues, and organs are largely composed of water. It maintains body temperature and aids in digestion. It also helps carry nutrients and oxygen to cells.

In the digestion process, water is crucial. It aids in the digestion of food in the stomach and makes it easier for nutrients to be absorbed in the small intestine. Constipation can be avoided, and proper digestion is supported by getting enough water.

Water aids in the body's natural detoxification process by aiding in the removal of waste and pollutants. It helps the liver and kidneys, which are in charge of filtering and getting rid of pollutants, work properly.

Drinking plenty of water can benefit cardiovascular health. It promotes appropriate blood pressure levels by maintaining blood volume. Dehydration increases the risk of heart-related problems and puts strain on the heart.

Water must be present in sufficient amounts for the kidneys to filter waste from the blood and generate urine. The incidence of kidney stones and urinary tract infections is lower with proper hydration.

"Water is the best liquid possible to cleanse the tissues. Pure water is the beverage which God provided to quench the thirst of animals and man. Drink freely of this hallowed fountain." "Counsels on Diet and Foods" by Ellen G. White, Chapter 7□

Sunlight

Natural sunshine exposure has advantages. In addition to providing vital nutrients, sunlight is beneficial for both physical and mental health. However, it is advised to use moderation and to avoid overexposure to the sun.

Due to its impact on the physiology of the body, research has revealed that exposure to sunlight has many positive effects on health. According to research, sunlight has the following significant advantages:

One of the most well-known advantages of sunlight is its function in the skin's production of vitamin D. Sunlight's UVB rays interact with the skin to produce vitamin D when they come into contact with it. This vitamin is crucial for bone health, calcium absorption, and general immunological performance. Rickets in children and osteoporosis in adults are two illnesses that can result from a vitamin D shortage.

Better Mood: Sunlight exposure is linked to better mental health and mood. Serotonin, a neurotransmitter referred to as the "feel-good" hormone, is stimulated by it. Serotonin has been related to positive emotions and sensations of relaxation. Seasonal affective disorder (SAD) and generalized symptoms of depression may be exacerbated by inadequate sunlight, particularly during the winter.

Regulated Circadian Rhythms: Exposure to daylight assists in regulating the circadian rhythm, the body's internal clock. For good sleep and awake, this regulation is essential. Enough daylight exposure during the day can enhance sleep quality and lower the incidence of sleep disorders.

Blood Pressure Control: According to some studies, exposure to sunlight may help lower blood pressure. In response to UVB radiation, the skin releases nitric oxide, which can dilate blood vessels and reduce blood pressure. To minimize overexposure and the hazards that come with it, sun exposure must be moderated.

> "Many who are sick might recover health by outdoor life. Through proper exercise, the living machinery, like a well-constructed engine, is kept in action. The good circulation of the blood through the muscles and extremities of the body induces health." "Counsels on Health" by Ellen G. White, Chapter 28,□

Above, we see the encouragement of outdoor activities like living and working out in the sunshine and fresh air for health improvement. While engaging in outdoor activities, exposure to the sun has advantages for both physical and mental well-being.

Moderation

Temperance, or moderation in everything, encourages people to refrain from overindulging in food, drinks, and other harmful habits while putting an emphasis on maintaining balance in all areas of life, which is crucial for good health.

There is a link between temperance and physical health. Temperance is a way to respect the body, which is the temple of God. People can preserve the health necessary to carry out their obligations by leading moderate lifestyles and eating habits. Dietary moderation should be practiced especially a plant-based, nutritious diet while cautioning against overindulgence.

Temperance enables individuals to develop a personal moral character. To achieve success and be valuable in helping others, one must possess self-control and moderation. Individuals can escape the ethical and moral challenges brought on by intemperance and excess by exercising self-control and abstaining from indulgence.

"The doctrine of Christian temperance must be lived out, and this will require of everyone who follows Jesus that he shall be temperate in all things." "Counsels on Diet and Foods" by Ellen G. White, Chapter 25,□

Fresh Air

Proper ventilation and access to fresh air is vital to sustain the human body. The lungs are the major organs through which gas exchange occurs. Oxygen is taken in through the nostrils and utilized in the body while carbon dioxide is exhaled back out.

There are several advantages of fresh air for both physical and mental health. The following are some major benefits of breathing in fresh air:

The concentration of oxygen in fresh air is higher, and oxygen is necessary for the body's cellular functions. Consuming enough oxygen promotes the generation of energy, cognitive function, and general vigor.

Inhaling clean air might assist in clearing the respiratory system. It can lessen the chance of developing respiratory conditions like allergies, asthma, and bronchitis. The elimination of pollutants and poisons from the lungs by breathing in fresh air is another benefit.

The immune system's performance can be improved by exposure to fresh air. More white blood cells are produced by the body as a result, which is important for fighting off diseases and infections.

Better blood circulation through exposure to fresh air helps make sure that oxygen-rich blood reaches every region of the body. Lower blood pressure and improved cardiovascular health may result from this.

Before going to bed, take a deep breath of fresh air to promote better sleep. The body's circadian cycle is regulated by fresh air, which lowers the likelihood of sleep problems.

Consider spending time outside in natural settings, opening windows for ventilation, and taking part in outdoor activities that promote deep breathing to get the benefits of fresh air. Maintaining general health and well-being requires regular exposure to fresh air.

Adequate Rest

Rest is important for sustaining physical, mental, and emotional health in a variety of ways. It is also important for preserving overall health and well-being. Here are some benefits of sleep:

For bodily recuperation and regeneration, sleep is crucial. The body may focus its efforts on mending and regrowing tissues, muscles, and cells when it is sleeping. This procedure is essential for recovery after illnesses, exercises, and injuries.

An immune system that is healthy needs to sleep. The body creates cytokines while you sleep, substances that help fight inflammation and infections. A healthy immune response must be maintained by getting regular, quality sleep.

Getting enough sleep lowers stress and fosters emotional health. The brain analyses and consolidates emotions and experiences while we sleep, which makes it simpler to handle daily challenges.

Hormone balance is supported by sleep. Particularly during sleep, hormones that influence development, metabolism, stress response, and appetite are regulated. Health problems and hormone abnormalities can result from disturbed sleep patterns.

For emotional stability and mental well-being, sleep is essential. The brain processes emotions and maintains psychological well-being during sleeping and relaxing. Chronic sleep loss is associated with a higher risk of mood disorders like anxiety and sadness.

Rest is an essential part of living a healthy lifestyle. It promotes general vitality, mental health, emotional resiliency, and physical recuperation. Making rest a priority through getting enough sleep, unwinding, and managing stress is essential for preserving good health and reaching a higher standard of living.

> "Nature needs time to recuperate her exhausted energies. In many cases if a person is given the opportunity to sleep several hours, he will awaken refreshed and invigorated." "Counsels on Diet and Foods" by Ellen G. White, Chapter 8,□

Trust in God

In every aspect of our lives, we should trust in God. He is in control of the world and so orders our steps in the direction we should go. Everyone on this earth has a purpose in this life. We should pray for direction in knowing what tasks we are meant to accomplish. We tend to deviate from God's will by not following his commandments and bringing more trouble to ourselves. Prayer and reading the Word is the key to knowing the path God has for us. Let us make it a part of our duty to search the scriptures and to daily have personal communion with God. This should be our desire.

"Those who walk in the path of obedience will meet opposition, and will have trials of their faith; but this is all essential to bring out their true character. You should ever hold the assurance that God is leading you." "Testimonies for the Church" by Ellen G. White, Volume 1□

What does God require us to remember?

Remember ye the law of Moses my servant, which I commanded unto him in Horeb for all Israel, with the statutes and judgments. Behold, I will send you Elijah the prophet before the coming of the great and dreadful day of the Lord: And he shall turn the heart of the fathers to the children, and the heart of the children to their fathers, lest I come and smite the earth with a curse. Mal 4:4-6

Note

In the 10 commandments, God reminds us that we should remember the sabbath day to keep it holy. Knowing that the sabbath was not done away with. Likewise, we are commissioned, to remember the law given to Moses with the statutes and judgments. This was given in Malachi which gives us the scene of christ when he comes back the third time after the millennium to destroy the wicked.

How did Abraham obey God's voice?

Because that Abraham obeyed my voice, and kept my charge, my commandments, my statutes, and my laws. Gen 26:5.

NOTE:

Here Abraham followed God's commandments, statutes, and laws. This showed how obedient he was to God's charge. To have a close walk with God and to understand his will for our lives we need to obey his commands and study his word. With constant communion with him, he will reveal to us the path to go. Abraham was promised that he would be the father of a great nation. He showed faith by obeying God's voice.

Is the descent of the Holy Spirit connected to God's statutes?

Then will I sprinkle clean water upon you, and ye shall be clean: from all your filthiness, and from all your idols, will I cleanse you. A new heart also will I give you, and a new spirit will I put within you: and I will take away the stony heart out of your flesh, and I will give you an heart of flesh. And I will put my spirit within you, and cause you to walk in my statutes, and ye shall keep my judgments, and do them. Ezekiel 36:25-27.

Note

The people of Israel are promised spiritual regeneration and renewal in this text. God will purify the people of their sins and give them a new heart and spirit, according to this verse. God has promised to sprinkle pure water on them, wash away their old, hard hearts, and replace them with new hearts that are receptive to God's will. This renewal will result from these actions. The passage continues by saying that God will give them His Spirit, which will allow them to obey Him and live as He commands.

Overall, this passage gives the people of Israel a message of optimism and the promise of a fresh start through spiritual regeneration and renewal.

What did Moses say the children of Israel should hear?

And Moses called all Israel, and said unto them, Hear, O Israel, the statutes and judgments which I speak in your ears this day, that ye may learn them, and keep, and do them. The Lord our God made a covenant with us in Horeb. Deut 5:1,2

Note

The children of Isreal were to listen and understand God's law. It was to be a part of their lives.

"God's favor toward Israel had always been conditional on their obedience. At the foot of Sinai, the hosts of Israel had entered into covenant relation with God as his "peculiar treasure ... above all people." Exodus 19:5They were to be to him "a kingdom of priests, and an holy nation." Solemnly they had promised to follow in the path of obedience. "All that the Lord hath spoken we will do," they said. And when, a few days afterward, God's law was spoken from Sinai, and additional instruction in the form of statutes and judgments was communicated through Moses, the Israelites with one voice again promised, "All the words which the Lord hath said will we do." Exodus 24:3. [2]

What is the meaning of the testimonies and statutes and judgments?

And when thy son asketh thee in time to come, saying, what mean the testimonies, and the statutes, and the judgments, which the Lord our God hath commanded you. Then thou shalt say unto thy son, we were Pharaoh's bondmen in Egypt; and the Lord brought us out of Egypt with a mighty hand...and the Lord commanded us to do all these statutes, to fear the Lord our God, for our good always, that he might preserve us alive, as it is at this day. Deut 6:20-24

Note

The passage states that if a child approaches their parent and inquires about the significance of God's laws and commandments. In response, the parent explains the significance of these instructions and emphasizes the necessity of diligently adhering to them. The passage ends by promising the Israelites long life and prosperity in the land that God has given them if they follow his commands.

Is prohibition of drinking alcohol a statute?

Do not drink wine nor strong drink, thou, nor thy sons with thee, when ye go into the tabernacle of the congregation, lest ye die: it shall be a statute forever throughout your generations. Lev 10:9

Note

The passage outlines the precise directions that God gave to Aaron, Israel's high priest, and his sons regarding how they were to behave while performing their duties in the tabernacle. They must abstain from alcohol before entering the tabernacle, in order to be able to differentiate between what is holy and what is not. The verse continues by stating that the ban on drinking while serving is an eternal law for all Israelite generations. The main focus of the passage is set on the value of being sober and completely present while serving as well as the lasting significance of the instructions given to Aaron and his offspring.

How long should we keep God's statutes and commandments?

That thou mightest fear the Lord thy God, to keep all his statutes and his commandments, which I command thee, thou, and thy son, and thy son's son, all the days of thy life; and that thy days may be prolonged. Deut 6:2

Note

The statutes were not only for biblical times and then to be done away with. The whole family was to keep these statutes and it was to be done all the days of our lives so that our days are prolonged.

"The teaching which has become so widespread that the divine statutes are no longer binding upon men, is the same as idolatry in its effect upon the morals of the people. Those who seek to lessen the claims of God's holy law are striking directly at the foundation of the government of families and nations. Religious parents, failing to walk in his statutes, do not command their household to keep the way of the Lord. The law of God is not made the rule of life. The children, as they make homes of their own, feel under no obligation to teach their children what they themselves have never been taught. And this is why there are so many godless families; this is why depravity is so deep and widespread." [3]

What is the statute regarding fat or blood?

And the priest shall burn them upon the altar: it is the food of the offering made by fire for a sweet savor: all the fat is the Lord's.It shall be a perpetual statute for your generations throughout all your dwellings, that ye eat neither fat nor blood.Lev 3:16-17

Note

Here we see the guidelines for consuming animal sacrifice blood and fat are laid out. The passage forbids the consumption of any blood, stating that it is a sacred symbol of life and must not be consumed. The fat of the animal that is sacrificed pertains to the Lord and must not be eaten. Anyone who breaks these laws will be expelled from the Israelite society. Overall, the prohibitions on the consumption of animal fat and blood, highlight their sacred and symbolic importance in the Israelites' religious rituals.

What did the Israelites have to do to keep the diseases away from them?

And said, if thou wilt diligently hearken to the voice of the Lord thy God, and wilt do that which is right in his sight, and wilt give ear to his commandments, and keep all his statutes, I will put none of these diseases upon thee, which I have brought upon the Egyptians: for I am the Lord that healeth thee. Ex15:26

NOTE:

In order for the Israelites to not be afflicted by the same diseases that were affecting the Egyptians, they were to keep God's commandments and statutes. Embedded in the statutes are health laws that were important for the Israelites to follow. These health laws are relevant today.

What should we do in order for us to prosper?

And keep the charge of the Lord thy God, to walk in his ways, to keep his statutes, and his commandments, and his judgments, and his testimonies, as it is written in the law of Moses, that thou mayest prosper in all that thou doest, and whithersoever thou turnest thyself: 1Kings2:3

Note

This verse is a portion of the instructions King David gives to his son Solomon, who will take over as king after him. David exhorts Solomon to observe the Lord's commands as stated in the Law of Moses and to follow the Lord. David stresses the value of following God's commands and says that if Solomon does so, he will be successful in everything he does. The passage emphasizes how crucial it is to follow God's instructions in order to benefit from his blessings and stay away from the adverse consequences of disobedience.

What does Moses do when the people come unto him to enquire of God?

And Moses said unto his father-in-law because the people come unto me to enquire of God: When they have a matter, they come unto me; and I judge between one and another, and I do make them know the statutes of God, and his laws.Ex18:15, 16

NOTE

It was Moses's responsibility to inform the Israelites of God's Law and commandments. Whenever there was discord among them and they needed direction in what course to take. They were reminded of the statutes and laws that they were to keep.

What did God tell Aaron about strong drink?

Do not drink wine nor strong drink, thou, nor thy sons with thee, when ye go into the tabernacle of the congregation, lest ye die: it shall be a statute forever throughout your generations: And that ye may put difference between holy and unholy, and between unclean and clean; And that ye may teach the children of Israel all the statutes which the Lord hath spoken unto them by the hand of Moses.Lev 10:9-11

NOTE

A major statute that Aaron and his sons were to abide by especially being priests in God's tabernacle was the prohibition of alcohol drinking. If it was vital for Aaron and his sons as priests to be holy before God by abstaining from drinking alcohol . We can still learn from this very important statute today.

What will happen to a man if he keeps God's statutes and judgments?

Ye shall therefore keep my statutes, and my judgments: which if a man do, he shall live in them: I am the Lord.Lev18:5

NOTE

This verse focuses on the fact that God orders the Israelites to obey His laws and ordinances and assures them that doing so will ensure their survival. The passage stresses the significance of following God's instructions because they are meant to lead His people towards a life of righteousness and submission to Him. Following God's laws results in a healthy relationship with Him, a life of blessing and satisfaction, and it also leads to a promise of life that extends beyond the physical to the spiritual. To live a life that is pleasing in God's sight. It is important for us to keep God's statutes, commandments, and Judgments. By following them you choose life. Blessings are available when choosing the path of God.

What statute is mentioned regarding the mingling of different types of clothes?

Ye shall keep my statutes. Thou shalt not let thy cattle gender with a diverse kind: thou shalt not sow thy field with mingled seed: neither shall a garment mingled of linen and woolen come upon thee. Lev 19:19

NOTE

God had certain specifications in his statutes that were to be followed. The mingling of clean and unclean was not permitted. Even certain garments were not to be mixed. Linen was to be worn especially for the priests going before God in the tabernacle. Wearing wool was not allowed as it would cause them to sweat.

What has God commanded the Israelites to do so the land does not spue them out?

Ye shall therefore keep all my statutes, and all my judgments, and do them: that the land, whither I bring you to dwell therein, spue you not out. Lev 20:22

Note

Where ever God lead the Israelites they were to follow his statutes, commandments, and judgments. The statutes involved the land resting every seventh year to keep the sabbatical. This is part of the agricultural Jewish economy. The judgments include blessings and curses. By walking in the commands of God the promised blessings were sure.

What should we do to dwell in the land of safety?

Wherefore ye shall do my statutes, and keep my judgments, and do them; and ye shall dwell in the land in safety. Lev 25:18

Note

No matter where we are in life, or whichever land we may reside in, it is important to keep God's statutes and judgments. We are reassured that we may dwell in safety in the land God has promised us.

What should we do for God to give us rain in due season?

If ye walk in my statutes, and keep my commandments, and do them; Then I will give you rain in due season and the land shall yield her increase and the trees of the field shall yield their fruit. Lev 26: 3-4

Note

The blessings are ours to have. It was already promised. The land will increase when rain is given in its season. When we follow God's statutes and his commandments this is promised to us. For six years we can prune, till the soil, and gather the fruits but in the seventh year, the land should rest.

What happens if we despise God's statutes?

And if ye shall despise my statutes, or if your soul abhor my judgments, so that ye will not do all my commandments, but that ye break my covenant: I also will do this unto you; I will even appoint over you terror, consumption and the burning ague, that shall consume the eyes and cause sorrow of heart: and ye shall sow your seed in vain, for your enemies shall eat it. Lev 26:15-16

Note

Follow God and you would have chosen life and the blessings that he has promised. If you despise his statutes and judgments, then you would have chosen the curse upon yourself.

Why were the Israelites punished?

The land also shall be left of them, and shall enjoy her Sabbaths, while she lieth desolate without them: and they shall accept of the punishment of their iniquity: because, even because they despised my judgments, and because their soul abhorred my statutes. Lev 26:43

Note

The Israelites were constantly disobeying God's statutes and commandments and judgments and so faced punishments for the wrong path they took.

What did the lord make between him and the children of Israel?

These are the statutes and judgments and laws, which the Lord made between him and the children of Israel in Mount Sinai by the hand of Moses. Lev 26:46

Note

The Lord had chosen the Israelites to be the keepers of the oracles of his statutes, commandments, and judgments. Their mission was to take it to the world but because of disobedience that did not happen. However, on the last day God's statutes, commandments, and judgments will be restored to the world.

What did God say the children of Israel should do to live?

Now, therefore, hearken, O Israel, unto the statutes and unto the judgments, which I teach you, for to do them, that ye may live, and go in and possess the land which the Lord God of your fathers giveth you. Deut 4:1

Note

To receive the blessings that God has for us it is important for us to obey his commands. The Israelites were commissioned to follow God's commands so that they may have a prosperous life as promised and live in peace in the promised land.

What was the Israelites wisdom and understanding in the sight of the nations?

Behold, I have taught you statutes and judgments, even as the Lord my God commanded me, that ye should do so in the land whither ye go to possess it. Keep therefore and do them; for this is your wisdom and your understanding in the sight of the nations, which shall hear all these statutes, and say, Surely this great nation is a wise and understanding people. Deut 4:5-6

Note

The Israelites when taught the statutes and judgments, were to live a life that was pleasing to God. By living according to God's command they were showing the world that God's ways are the best. They would be seen as wise in the sight of other nations and so would win others to Jesus.

Were there other nations that had the statutes and judgements besides the Israelites at that time?

And what nation is there so great, that hath statutes and judgments so righteous as all this law, which I set before you this day? Deut 4:8

Note

The Israelites were the chosen nation who were to keep God's statutes, commandments, and Judgments. God's mission was for the Isrealites to be an example to the world so God could be seen in their everyday lives. This was a powerful witness to the world.

What were the children of Israel to do when they possessed a new land?

And the Lord commanded me at that time to teach you statutes and judgments, that ye might do them in the land whither ye go over to possess it. Deut 4:14

Note

Before possessing a new land the children of Isreal were to be cognizant of the fact that the statutes Commandments and judgments were important and had to be followed in order for them to gain a blessing in the land that they would possess.

What were the Israelites to do to prolong their days?

Thou shalt keep therefore his statutes, and his commandments, which I command thee this day, that it may go well with thee, and with thy children after thee, and that thou mayest prolong thy days upon the earth, which the Lord thy God giveth thee, forever. Deut 4:40

Note

There were blessings to receive from God when they followed his statutes and commandments. Those blessings were also to be passed down from generation to generation If they continued to follow his law.

What shall Moses teach to the Israelites?

But as for thee, stand thou here by me, and I will speak unto thee all the commandments, and the statutes, and the judgments, which thou shalt teach them, that they may do them in the land which I give them to possess it. Deut 5:31

Note

Here again, is a promise given that involves being able to live in the blessings of God in the land that is promised on the condition that the commandments, statutes, and judgments of God are obeyed. It was Moses's commission to teach these commands to the Israelites so that each generation to come would know about them. Today they are even more vital for this generation.

What should we do to live?

And I gave them my statutes and showed them my judgments, which if a man does, he shall even live in them. Moreover, also I gave them my Sabbaths, to be a sign between me and them, that they might know that I am the Lord that sanctifies them. Ez 20:11, 12

Note

In order to live a life that is pleasing to God. Following the world's standard is not the way to go. God gave us his commandments, statutes, and judgments to follow. The Sabbath is a sign between God's people and himself. By following his commandments including the fourth "Remember the sabbath day to keep it holy six days though shall do they work but the seventh day is the sabbath of the lord thy God.' we are showing the world that we are obeying God's law.

What did the house of Israel do to cause God to pour his fury upon them?

But the house of Israel rebelled against me in the wilderness: they walked not in my statutes, and they despised my judgments, which if a man do, he shall even live in them; and my Sabbaths they greatly polluted: then I said, I would pour out my fury upon them in the wilderness, to consume them. Ez 20:13

Note

We serve a loving God that gives us our heart's desire if it is within his will. He only asks us to obey his commands. Why is it so hard to obey? Like a loving parent telling his/her child not to play with matches or he/she will burn themselves. The command was given for their own protection. Likewise when God gives us commands to obey It is for our own protection and love. The Sabbath was given to man not man for the Sabbath. In the passage, the Israelites greatly polluted that holy day and so they were punished for the same.

What did God give mankind as a sign between us and God?

I am the Lord your God; walk in my statutes, and keep my judgments, and do them, and hallow my Sabbaths; and they shall be a sign between me and you, that ye may know that I am the Lord your God. Ez 20:19-20.

Note

"The power that created all things is the power that re-creates the soul in His own likeness. To those who keep holy the Sabbath day it is the sign of sanctification. True sanctification is harmony with God, oneness with Him in character. It is received through obedience to those principles that are the transcript of His character. And the Sabbath is the sign of obedience. He who from the heart obeys the fourth commandment will obey the whole law. He is sanctified through obedience." [4]

What keeps the heart rejoicing and enlightens the eye?

The statutes of the LORD are right, rejoicing the heart: the commandment of the LORD is pure, enlightening the eyes. Ps19:8

Note

"In every generation and in every land the true foundation for character building has been the same—the principles contained in the word of God. The only safe and sure rule is to do what God says. "The statutes of the Lord are right," and "he that doeth these things shall never be moved." It was with the word of God that the apostles met the false theories of their day, saying, "Other foundation can no man lay than that is laid." [5]

Is Tithing a Statute?

And behold, I have given the children of Levi all the tenth in Israel for an inheritance, for their service which they serve, even the service of the tabernacle of the congregation.Neither must the children of Israel henceforth come nigh the tabernacle of the congregation, lest they bear sin, and die. But the Levites shall do the service of the tabernacle of the congregation, and they shall bear their iniquity: it shall be a statute for ever throughout your generations, that among the children of Israel they have no inherita nce.Num 18:21-23

Note

The duties and rights of the Levites, who were designated as priests to work in the tabernacle, are described in this passage. In order to acknowledge the Levites for their work in the tabernacle, God commanded Moses to give them a share of the tithes that the Israelites gave. The tithes were given to the Levites as a means of providing for themselves and their families rather than a part of the property. The passage also highlights how crucial the Levites' service to the Lord is and how seriously they must carry out their responsibilities in the tabernacle.

What are the promises God gives us regarding tithing?

Will a man rob God? Yet ye have robbed me. But ye say, Wherein have we robbed thee? In tithes and offerings.Ye are cursed with a curse: for ye have robbed me, even this whole nation.Bring ye all the tithes into the storehouse, that there may be meat in mine house, and prove me now herewith, saith the Lord of hosts, if I will not open you the windows of heaven, and pour you out a blessing, that there shall not be room enough to receive it. Mal 3:8-10

Note

This verse emphasizes the value of paying offerings to God. The text accuses the Israelites of robbing God by failing to give offerings and tithes. The passage states that those who give their tithes to God will receive blessings, saying that God will open the windows of heaven and pour out blessings that are impossible to enumerate. This passage primarily focuses on the rewards of faithful obedience to God and the significance of offering Him what is due.

What did God say regarding clean and unclean?

And that ye may put difference between holy and unholy, and between unclean and clean; and that ye may teach the children of Israel all the statutes which the Lord hath spoken unto them by the hand of Moses. Lev 10:10-11

Note

God gave Aaron, the high priest of Israel, and his sons precise instructions about how they were to behave while working in the tabernacle. They must make a distinction between what is holy and what is ordinary, as well as between what is unclean and what is clean, and they must impart to the Israelites all the laws that God has commanded them. Aaron and his sons have been designated to serve as priests and to take accountability for any wrongdoing that may arise from their failure to adhere to God's directions. In general, this passage highlights the significance of the priests' position in instructing and directing the Israelites in holiness-related matters as well as the repercussions of failing to carry out their responsibilities.

Are the feasts a statute?

And on the fifteenth day of the same month is the feast of unleavened bread unto the Lord: seven days ye must eat unleavened bread. In the first day ye shall have an holy convocation: ye shall do no servile work therein.But ye shall offer an offering made by fire unto the Lord seven days: in the seventh day is an holy convocation: ye shall do no servile work therein....And ye shall eat neither bread, nor parched corn, nor green ears, until the selfsame day that ye have brought an offering unto your God: it shall be a statute forever throughout your generations in all your dwellings. Lev23:6-8, 14

Note

The seven-day festival that succeeds Passover is referred to in these verses as the Feast of Unleavened Bread. The Israelites are instructed to consume only yeast-free bread during this period, as well as to purge their homes of all yeast. It is forbidden to perform any labor on the first and last days of the festival, which are regarded as holy days.

Why did God take away the Kingdom from Solomon?

Wherefore the Lord said unto Solomon, forasmuch as this is done of thee, and thou hast not kept my covenant and my statutes, which I have commanded thee, I will surely rend the kingdom from thee, and will give it to thy servant. 1Kings 11:11

Note

In this passage, God forewarns King Solomon about the events that would transpire during his rule and the repercussions of his disobedience to God's covenant and statutes. Solomon is highly blessed by God, but he disobeys Him and turns to other gods. God then informs Solomon that he will lose the kingdom and it will be handed to someone else.

What did Solomon have to do for God to lengthen his days?

And if thou wilt walk in my ways, to keep my statutes and my commandments, as thy father David did walk, then I will lengthen thy days. 1Kings 3:14

Note

Here, King Solomon hears from God, who assures him that if he obeys His instructions and walks in His ways, He will bestow upon him great knowledge and understanding, riches, and honor. The verse focuses on the value of pursuing wisdom and doing God's will, as well as the benefits that can result from doing so.

What should we do for our hearts to be perfect with God?

Let your heart therefore be perfect with the Lord our God, to walk in his statutes, and to keep his commandments, as at this day. 1Kings 8:61

Note

King Solomon ends his dedication prayer for the temple he had constructed for the Lord in this verse. Then, after thanking the Lord for His steadfastness and promising to walk before Him with a loyal heart, he prays for the Lord to be with his people and to uphold their cause and right. The verse focuses on the value of loyalty and fidelity to God and the necessity of seeking His presence and blessing in all areas of life.

Who gives wisdom and understanding?

Only the Lord give thee wisdom and understanding, and give thee charge concerning Israel, that thou mayest keep the law of the Lord thy God. Then shalt thou prosper, if thou takest heed to fulfil the statutes and judgments which the Lord charged Moses with concerning Israel be strong, and of good courage; dread not, nor be dismayed. 1Chron 22:12-13

Note

This verse emphasizes how king David chooses his son Solomon to succeed him as the ruler and construct a temple for the Lord. Solomon is urged by David to be brave and strong, to follow the Lord's instructions, and to construct the sanctuary for the Lord with great care and attention to detail. In addition, David pledges to provide the necessary funding for the temple's building and asks the Lord to support and guide Solomon in his endeavors. The passage emphasizes the value of abiding by God's instructions, exercising strength and bravery, and making the most of one's resources for God's honor.

Why did David say it was good for him to be afflicted?

It is good for me that I have been afflicted; that I might learn thy statutes .Ps.119:71

Note

This verse demonstrates how the psalmist considers the trials and tribulations he has endured throughout his existence. He admits that these challenges have been advantageous for him because they have allowed him to develop his faith and his comprehension of God's laws. The verse implies that hardships and adversity can have a beneficial impact on our lives by fostering our capacity for resilience, wisdom, and a closer connection to God.

What did God communicated to the Isrealites on Mount Sinai?

Thou camest down also upon mount Sinai, and spakest with them from heaven, and gavest them right judgments, and true laws, good statutes and commandments. Neh 9:13☐

Note:

This verse emphasizes what happened at Mount Sinai when God appeared to the Israelites and spoke with them. It highlights how God gave them righteous laws, judgments, good statutes, and commands. During their time at Mount Sinai God gave the Israelites a set of just and true commands for living in accordance with His will which should be followed throughout their generations.☐

How does one become blessed and fruitful?

In that I command thee this day to love the Lord thy God, to walk in his ways, and to keep his commandments and his statutes and his judgments, that thou mayest live and multiply: and the Lord thy God shall bless thee in the land whither thou goest to possess it. Deut 30:16 □

Note

This text exhorts people to follow God's commandments and statutes. It emphasizes that one can have a blessed and fruitful life by sincerely and devotedly adhering to these heavenly prescriptions. In essence, it promotes the link between following God's commands faithfully and the rewards that come as a result.

What does God command us to observe here?

Therefore shall ye observe all my statutes, and all my judgments, and do them: I am the Lord.Lev19:37

NOTE

The Israelites were given these commands to follow throughout their generation. We are also commanded to keep his statutes and judgments and to observe them as children of God throughout our generations.

Should a stranger who stays with you keep the statutes?

Ye shall therefore keep my statutes and my judgments, and shall not commit any of these abominations; neither any of your own nation, nor any stranger that sojourneth among you: Lev 18:26

NOTE

What was given to the Israelites to keep was also extended to the strangers who lodged with them. The statutes, commandments, and judgments are applicable to everyone.

What are the judges required to do ?

And what cause soever shall come to you of your brethren that dwell in your cities, between blood and blood, between law and commandment, statutes and judgments, ye shall even warn them that they trespass not against the Lord, and so wrath come upon you, and upon your brethren: this do, and ye shall not trespass.2 Chron 19:10

Note

This verse instructs judges and leaders to faithfully uphold the law and administer justice fairly, making sure they follow the principles and commandments of the Lord, in cases of conflict or conflicts among the people. This verse focuses on the significance of upholding justice and avoiding conduct that would incur God's wrath or fury.

What blessings are promised here?

The Lord shall command the blessing upon thee in thy storehouses, and in all that thou settest thine hand unto; and he shall bless thee in the land which the Lord thy God giveth thee. Duet 28:8

Note

This verse is a part of a passage in which God offers the Israelites rewards in exchange for their unwavering obedience to His laws. It indicates that God will command His blessings to be upon them in everything they do, whether it is in their businesses, their fields, or their regular activities. As long as they continue to follow His laws, it guarantees them God's favor and success in all of their endeavors.

The Ten Commandments

1. Thou shalt have none other gods before me.

2. Thou shalt not make thee any graven image, or any likeness of anything that is in heaven above, or that is in the earth beneath, or that is in the waters beneath the earth:Thou shalt not bow down thyself unto them, nor serve them: for I the Lord thy God am a jealous God, visiting the iniquity of the fathers upon the children unto the third and fourth generation of them that hate me,And shewing mercy unto thousands of them that love me and keep my commandments.

3. Thou shalt not take the name of the Lord thy God in vain: for the Lord will not hold him guiltless that taketh his name in vain.

4. Remember the sabbath day, to keep it holy. Six days shalt thou labour, and do all thy work: But the seventh day is the sabbath of the Lord thy God: in it thou shalt not do any work, thou, nor thy son, nor thy daughter, thy manservant, nor thy maidservant, nor thy cattle, nor thy stranger that is within thy gates: For in

six days the Lord made heaven and earth, the sea, and all that in them is, and rested the seventh day: wherefore the Lord blessed the sabbath day and hallowed it.

5. Honour thy father and thy mother: that thy days may be long upon the land which the Lord thy God giveth thee.

6. Thou shalt not kill.

7. Thou shalt not commit adultery.

8. Thou shalt not steal.

9. Thou shalt not bear false witness against thy neighbour.

10. Thou shalt not covet thy neighbor's house; thou shalt not covet thy neighbor's wife, nor his manservant, nor his maidservant, nor his ox, nor his ass, nor any thing that is thy neighbor's. Ex 20 :3-17

The Judgments – Blessings

5 Blessings

And it shall come to pass, if thou shalt hearken diligently unto the voice of the Lord thy God, to observe and to do all his commandments which I command thee this day, that the Lord thy God will set thee on high above all nations of the earth: And all these blessings shall come on thee, and overtake thee, if thou shall hearken unto the voice of the Lord thy God.

1. Blessed shalt thou be in the city and blessed shalt thou be in the field.

2. Blessed shall be the fruit of thy body, and the fruit of thy ground, and the fruit of thy cattle, the increase of thy kine, and the flocks of thy sheep.

3. Blessed shall be thy basket and thy store.

4. Blessed shalt thou be when thou comest in and blessed shalt thou be when thou goest out.

5. The Lord shall cause thine enemies that rise up against thee to be smitten before thy face: they shall come out against thee one way, and flee before thee seven ways. Deut28:1-7

REFERENCES

1. MDPI and ACS Style

   Kahleova, H.; Levin, S.; Barnard, N. Cardio-Metabolic Benefits of Plant-Based Diets. Nutrients 2017, 9, 848. https://doi.org/10.3390/nu9080848

2. https://m.egwwritings.org/en/book/1965.4439#4439

3. https://m.egwwritings.org/en/book/10.817#817

4. https://m.egwwritings.org/en/book/19.2010#2010

5. https://m.egwwritings.org/en/book/127.2074#2074